IMPRINTS OF TIME

IMPRINTS OF TIME:

The Art of Geology

Bradford B. Van Diver

MOUNTAIN PRESS PUBLISHING COMPANY
MISSOULA, 1988

COVER: Sculptured granite
on the Brittany shore, Perros-Guirec France

LIBRARY OF CONGRESS CATALOGING-IN-PUBLICATION DATA

Van Diver, Bradford B.
Imprints of time; the art of geology Bradford B. Van Diver.
p.   cm.
ISBN 0-87842-215-3
1. Photography—Landscapes. 2. Geology—Pictorial works.
I. Title.
TR660. 5.V36 1988
779'.36'0924—dc19   87-19390 CIP

Printed in Singapore by Singapore National Printers Ltd through Palace Press

Mountain Press Publishing Company
2016 Strand Avenue • P.O. Box 2399
Missoula, Montana 59806
(406) 728-1900

Dedication

For all those with deep appreciation and awe of Earth, but especially for one, Tony Dunn — friend, student, teacher — whose brief life celebrated this wonder. May his kindred, adventurous spirit forever dwell among the Alaskan mountains he so deeply loved.

Table of Contents

Lhotse Shar, Everest Group, Nepal

The Essence of Geologic Art

THE ART OF GEOLOGY is Nature's handiwork. It is landscapes, rocks, lavas, sediments, soils, minerals, fossils, glaciers, rivers. It is the art of the possible, for in Nature, almost anything is possible. It is dynamic art, for in the context of geologic time, it is everchanging. It comes in all sizes, from colossal to submicroscopic, with great beauty at all levels. It is art with a fourth dimension — time. It is living art of inanimate substance, sensitive to time, day, season, weather, lighting.

The art of geology represents a delicate balance between forces of nature that create and forces that destroy. The solid, liquid, and gaseous components of Earth called lithosphere, hydrosphere, and atmosphere, are intimately mixed and interactive with each other and with a fourth component, the biosphere that encompasses all living matter. All four spheres obey the same laws of physics and chemistry and therefore, automatically adjust to changing conditions by reaching a state of dynamic equilibrium. "Dynamic" is the key word here for Earth is in a constant state of flux. In the course of geologic time, whole worlds have been created and destroyed, over and over again.

The long-term behavior of streams illustrates the point. When mountains rise, streams flow down their sides. Each stream gradient is adjusted until the water velocity of each part of the channel is just sufficient to move the materials supplied to it from the valley sides and from upstream. The gradient is steep near the headwaters because large boulders must move there, and gentler farther downstream, in part because the boulders are broken down by the time they get there. The gentlest gradients are near the mouth, where only the finest sediments need move. At this stage the stream is in a state of dynamic equilibrium in which the channel slowly, systematically flattens as the mountains wear down. In this case the mountain uplift represents the forces that create, and the stream and its partner in crime, gravity, are the destructive forces. The finely sculptured mountains are products of millions of years of conflict.

Time is surely Nature's friend in art. The extreme slowness of some of Nature's handiwork is graphically illustrated in two sets of photographs of the canyonlands of the Colorado River taken 97 years apart. The first set was taken by E. O. Beaman during John Wesley Powell's second trip down the river in 1871, the second by a U. S. Geological Survey team in 1968 with the purpose of assessing visual changes in the landscape. The team was able to find more than 90% of Beaman's photographic viewpoints and rephotograph the same scenes. The similarity of the paired photographs is simply beyond belief! Almost no changes can be detected in the gross features, and only minute changes in detail: the texture of a talus block appears slightly more weathered, or the river has shifted a little and a sandbar appears in the second photograph where there was none in the first. If the changes wrought by 97 years are nearly invisible to us, then imagine how long it took the Colorado River to cut through the 4-mile thick layercake of rock now exposed in the canyonlands and in the process to create spectacles of such awesome magnitude and splendor? The extreme slowness of some geologic processes, both on and within the earth, contributes immensely to the perfection and beauty of its artwork.

Above all, geologic art is unique because every element of it is a document of Earth history. "Reading the rocks" is what geologists do, but this world is not theirs alone. With a little background, anyone can develop the skill. Once begun, images of earth as it was blend with the physical world of now, and invariably enhance the perception and appreciation of its beauty. Earth becomes a tremendously exciting place — no matter where you are.

Reading the rocks requires and promotes an appreciation of geologic time, the time between formation of Earth and now. The earth is at least 4600 million years old. It is impossible to comprehend such a large span of time; we can't relate to it with our human clocks that deal in days, weeks, months, years — even millenia are too short. The geologic clock ticks away a million years at a time. In its long history Earth has experienced monumental changes, many of which required hundreds of millions of years to complete. To read the rocks in the chronological order of their formation is to compress history to a more human scale, in which Earth is seen as an almost living being. It's a vigorous world in which whole continents move over its surface like floating islands, ocean basins open and close and open again, mountain ranges rise, wear down, and rise again, and shallow seas alternately flood and retreat from the continental interiors. In the context of geologic time, everything is constantly changing, including all of the geologic phenomena that can be framed in the camera. For me, this realization is a perpetual source of wonder, exhilaration, and anticipation.

This is the essence of geologic art.

Silver Grotto in
Redwall limestone,
Grand Canyon
Arizona

Canyonlands

Canyonlands

SEEING IT FOR THE FIRST TIME took my breath away. Intellectually I was well-prepared; but I knew from that first moment that textbooks and pictures could never capture the spirit of it. You have to experience the Grand Canyon with your whole being to appreciate it. Standing at the rim of this enormous chasm is like being at the edge of the world, an impression reinforced by the flatness of the plateau over which you have come to reach this abrupt ending. When you arrive, it is as if the ground before you has suddenly collapsed. The immensity and grandeur of the panorama overwhelm you. Your first impulse is to look down, to follow the profile of the canyon wall from the Kaibab cliff that drops away beneath your feet, down across the procession of cliff, terrace, cliff, terrace, cliff — down and down and down, as the details of the rock sculpture blend together. You find a place where you can see beyond the last and broadest terrace, the Tonto platform, into the sombre, purplish-black inner gorge of the river. The river — that inexorable progenitor of this grand scene — appears from here like nothing more than a twisted thread, insignificant and impotent, tucked among the mesas, buttes, castles, thrones, temples, pinnacles, pillars, plateaus, gorges — all that intricate maze of finely crafted rock. Let your eye trace back up along the similar steps of the other side, up and up until it reaches the level of the opposite rim, wrapped in the purplish haze of distance. Follow the rim rocks way over to the left and right as far as you can see. The stupendous size of the canyon leaves you in a state of shock and disbelief.

Seeing it once is not enough, for unlike a picture on the wall, the Grand Canyon is an everchanging work of art. If you view it a thousand times, you will see as many different canyons. Aptly described as a "stone rainbow" the many colorful layers of rocks — reds, browns, oranges, and yellows — are most intense in the tinted light of sunrise or sunset. At midday, especially in spring, there are the subtle greens of vegetation on the Tonto platform and in some of the side canyons where water periodically wets the soil. Colorful cliffs stand out sharply against the white of winter snow. Each season, each day, each hour brings a new picture.

If the spectacle of the Grand Canyon is awesome, its geological story, much of it decipherable in the view from the canyon rim, is mind-boggling. The combination is overwhelming.

The Grand Canyon is one of the greatest geologic exposures in the world. It is like a huge book of earth history lying on its side, with page one at the bottom. At the top, you might add the words "to be continued" rather than "the end;" for you need only move back over the plateau a few miles from the rim to the Vermillion Cliffs in order to pick up the story in yet higher pages. And even they are not the end; farther back, more pages — and so on. The story continues in the canyonlands to the north. In Zion Canyon are essentially the same sedimentary rock beds as those of the Vermillion Cliffs. Bryce Canyon exposes higher, younger beds yet. Geologists have determined that all of these layers once covered the entire area, adding as much as three miles to the thickness of the rocks now exposed in Grand Canyon before the Colorado River went to work on it. All therefore, are part of a colossal canyonlands. The Colorado River and tributaries carved them from a slowly risng plateau, and it may someday reduce the landscape to a surface of little relief at sea level. In that sense, the canyonlands are geologically youthful.

All rocks are clues to larger events of plate tectonics that provided the environment for their formation. Widespread metamorphic and igneous intrusive rocks, like those of the Vishnu group exposed in the inner gorge of the Grand Canyon, speak eloquently of continental collisions. The original materials were similar to some of the flat-lying sedimentary strata of the upper canyon until continental collision crumpled, metamorphosed, and partially melted them 1700 million years ago, creating high mountains along the edge of ancestral North America.

Mountains are temporary landscapes subject to geologically rapid destruction by erosion. The higher they rise, the faster the erosion. Once the ancient Vishnu mountains ceased to rise, erosion slowly leveled them, leaving only the core rocks we now see in the inner canyon. Geologists call the erosional surface an unconformity; it represents missing pages of Earth history. This is one of the biggest unconformities in the world.

All of the enormous pile of sedimentary rock strata above the great unconformity of the Grand Canyon tell of relative plate tectonic calm, when North America was either merged with another continent, or it had split and was pulling away from it, or simply that this region was then in the continental interior far from active plate boundaries. Sedimentary rocks are also filing cabinets full of records of the earth environment at the time and place of their formation. Limestone, for example, is usually an outer continental shelf deposit; most shale means a shallower marine environment nearer shore; cross-bedded sandstone usually means continental deposition under shoreline or desert conditions. Stratified assemblages of sedimentary rocks stacked as they formed with the oldest on the bottom, report the progress of Earth history.

Above the Vishnu unconformity are two major groups of stratified rocks. The Grand Canyon group of late Precambrian age rests directly on the Vishnu group wherever erosional remnants of it remain. It consists of interbedded sedimentary and volcanic rocks in layers parallel to the unconformity, but nearly everywhere tilted and cut by steep block faults that extend downward into the Vishnu schists. It records, first, a long period of plate tectonic calm during which this region was near or below sea level and a site of deposition. Flat-lying strata piled up over the worn stumps of the Vishnu mountains until they achieved a total thickness of about 12,000 feet. Subsequent broad regional arching initiated a new erosional cycle and unconformity, and block-faulting similar to that of the modern Basin and Range province. Starting with an early version of the Grand Canyon, this cycle eventually reduced the land again to sea level, as the Colorado River and tributaries will almost certainly do in the far distant future.

Today, only wedges of the Grand Canyon group remain below the younger unconformity; elsewhere the basal beds of the Paleozoic sedimentary rock sequence rest directly on Vishnu schist, an unconformity that spans fully 1200 million years!

If anything, the story written in the flat-lying Paleozoic strata of the upper canyon walls is even more dramatic. It is a story that spans the Paleozoic era from beginning to end — with some missing pages caused by one major and several minor unconformities. The rocks are full of fossils that tell of rapidly proliferating and evolving life on Earth.

Trilobites are particularly notable and well-represented. This extinct marine crustacean, akin to the modern horseshoe crab, first entered the stage in the Cambrian period at the beginning of Paleozoic time, and its evolutionary descendants took their final bows at the conclusion of the era, never to appear again. During their 320 million year existence, trilobites dominated the sea, and then they suddenly disappeared forever. Incredibly, the scene from the Grand Canyon rim spans the entire evolutionary history of this remarkable creature, whose fossilized remains abound in many of the marine beds of the canyon walls.

You cannot, of course, see the trilobites or the many other fossils in the grand view from the canyon rim. But knowing of their presence and something about what they mean adds a fourth dimension — time — every bit equal to that of the images of advancing and retreating seas imprinted in the rocks themselves.

From the rim, what can you see of the history written in the rocks as distinguished from the more recent history of the erosion of the canyon? Actually, a great deal. The irregular erosional texture of the inner canyon clearly means metamorphic and igneous rocks with all their implications. The even stratification of the rocks above as clearly means sedimentary or volcanic, with an erosional unconformity above the ancient rocks below. The steps in the canyon walls indicate different rock types: cliffs are resistant sandstone or limestone; benches are less resistant shaley rocks. At the base of the Paleozoic section is a cliff-former. You can't tell from the rim whether it's sandstone or limestone, but a little background indicates that sandstone is more likely to lie directly above any unconformity. Transition from erosion to deposition occurs when the erosional surface is first flooded; a beach deposits sand, seldom limestone.

The Tonto platform is carved in shale, meaning deeper water deposition. Above that are cliffs of limestone, formed farther offshore beyond the muddy waters from rivers. The record visible in the erosional character alone is one of an advancing sea.

Continuing upward, there is a broad, relatively steep bench indicative of more shaley beds and a shallowing or retreating sea; their red color means a hot, dry climate at the time of deposition. Next is a massive buff-colored cliff whose color alone speaks of clean sandstone; it is a petrified sand dune layer with large cross-beds visible at closer range. The remaining section above is mostly limestone, culminating in the rimrock cliff — all marine deposits.

Thus, knowing something about the relationships between landscapes and rocks, and knowing how rocks form, enables you to see history in action in the Grand Canyon — or any other canyonlands.

And the story continues beyond the rim.

A wintery Grand Canyon
in early March,
as seen from the south rim

From the canyon rim
I stand witness to great events,
of growing mountains, earthquakes
and volcanic convulsions,
and to quieter times when jagged peaks
become rounded hills
and then no hills at all.

I swim in primordial seas
that invade the lowered land
among strange ancestors.
I, with some of them,
crawl upon the shore
to breathe my first air and
I watch as green invades the barrenness.

I wander among strange forests
that echo the screams
of fearful beasts.
They are there in the rocks, and I with them
for we are companions in time
from the same beginning.

Sunrise from the south rim

Beside what mighty canyon,
millenia hence,
will sentient spirit
stand bemused,
reflecting with awe and wonder
on millenia past?

Tonto Platform from the south rim, Grand Canyon

Kaibab limestone cliff at sunrise, Grand Canyon

At lower end of Marble Canyon, banded Redwall limestone cliff, Muav
limestone at left, Supai group above in background. Grand Canyon

The glories and the beauties of form, color, and sound unite in the Grand Canyon – forms unrivaled even by the mountains, colors that vie with sunsets, and sounds that span the diapason from tempest to tinkling raindrop, from cataract to bubbling fountain. But more: it is a vast district of country. Were it a valley plain it would make a state. It can be seen only in parts from hour to hour and from day to day and from week to week and from month to month. A year scarcely suffices to see it all. It has infinite variety, and no part is ever duplicated. Its colors, though many and complex at any instant, change with the ascending and declining sun; lights and shadows appear and vanish with the passing clouds, and the changing seasons mark their passage in changing colors. You cannot see the Grand Canyon in one view, as if it were a changeless spectacle from which a curtain might be lifted, but to see it you have to toil from month to month through its labyrinths. It is a region more difficult to traverse than the Alps or the Himalayas, but if strength and courage are sufficient for the task, by a year's toil a concept of sublimity can be obtained never again to be equaled on the hither side of Paradise.

John Wesley Powell, 1885

Shadowy Grand Canyon downstream from Marble Canyon

Alpenglow on Tapeats sandstone cliff seen from
Bright Angel Canyon, Grand Canyon,

Colorado River,
Grand Canyon

Monument Basin
from Grandview Point,
Canyonlands National Park, Utah

Shadowy canyonlands
from Grandview Point,
Canyonlands National Park, Utah

Badlands

Sunset in Badlands National Park, South Dakota

Badlands

THE BIZARRE LANDFORMS called badlands are, despite the uninviting name, Nature's masterpieces of water sculpture. They are deserts of a special kind, where rain is infrequent, the naked rocks are poorly consolidated and more or less uniform in their resistance to erosion, and runoff water washes away large amounts of sediment. They are formidable redoubts of stark beauty where the delicate balance between creation and decay, that distinguishes so much geologic art, is manifested in improbable "moonscapes" whose individual elements seem to defy gravity. Erosion is so rapid that the landforms can change perceptibly overnight as a result of a single cloudburst.

At Badlands National Park in South Dakota, weird shapes are etched into a plateau of soft sediments and volcanic ash, revealing colorful bands of flat-lying strata. The stratification adds immeasurably to the beauty of each scene, binding together all of its diverse parts. Viewed horizontally, individual beds are traceable from pinnacle to pinnacle, mound to mound, ridge to ridge, across the intervening ravines; the effect resembles a sculpture in several kinds of laminated hardwoods. Viewed from above, the bands curve in and out of the valleys like contour lines on a topographic map.

A geologic story is written in the rocks of Badlands National

Park, every bit as fascinating and colorful as their outward appearance. It is an account of 75 million years of accumulation with intermittent periods of erosion that began when the Rocky Mountains reared up in the West and spread sediments over vast expanses of the plains. The sand, silt, and clay, mixed and interbedded with volcanic ash, stacked up, layer upon flat-lying layer, until the pile was thousands of feet deep. In a final phase of volcanism as the uplift ended, white ash rained from the sky to frost the cake, completing the building stage.

During part of the period, in the Oligocene epoch, 40 - 25 million years ago, the region that is now the badlands supported many kinds of animals. The land was then lush, well-watered, and much warmer than now. The animals, mostly mammals, roamed the floodplains; many died in floods and were quickly buried in river sediments. Conditions for preservation were excellent; the Oligocene beds are one of the world's richest vertebrate fossil sites, though they represent only a short segment of Earth history.

Broad regional uplift raised the land about 5 million years ago and initiated the erosion that created the badlands. The White River, which now flows west to east 5 or 10 miles south of the badlands, eroded a scarp, the beginning of what is now called the Wall. Numerous small streams and rills furrowed the scarp face and eventually intersected to create the badlands topography. Each rainstorm over the next 5 million years chewed away at the Wall, making its crest recede northward away from the river as its base followed suit.

This is an old story in the arid and semi-arid regions of the West. It always happens in rocks that are relatively non-resistant to erosion, and it always starts with a scarp. At Badlands National Park, the White River produced the scarp; in many parts of the southwest, in the Basin and Range province, vertical fault movements provided the necessary relief. Once begun, parallel slope retreat maintains this badlands erosion. Gullying first wears the face of the scarp back to a stable, and usually quite steep, angle of slope. The erosive energy of runoff water concentrates at the base of the scarp to undercut and oversteepen the slope while minute adjustments bring it back to a stable incline. Another result is a gently sloping surface called a desert plain that extends from the foot of the badlands, with an abrupt angular break at their juncture. The desert plain is an erosional surface thinly veneered with sediments from the badlands; thus it is also a surface of transportation.

The physical character of the Badlands varies considerably according to the nature of the materials. For example, the frosting of volcanic ash at Badlands National Park succumbs quickly as the Wall advances northward into the upper plain — the original land surface — exposing the more durable underlying beds of the Brule formation. Nature's answer to greater resistance is to carve steeper slopes, resulting here in incredibly slender spires above knife-sharp ridges and intricately creased slopes. Deeper into the layercake, the more rounded ridges and spurs, and gentler slopes, reflect the lesser resistance of the Chadron formation. Numerous "islands" of Chadron mudstone dot the desert plain in front of the Wall. They look like nothing more than mud-mounds, except for striking color-banding which matches perfectly that of the base of the Wall. They are remnants, soon to be gone, of the earlier, ever-changing badland left stranded as the Wall receded.

Badlands National Park,
South Dakota

Suspended in time,
   awesome, pointed moon-forms,
   knife-ribbed and cat-clawed
   upon pedestals of clay
   spear the desert sky,
   monuments to the destruction
   of an illustrious past.

The strata cannot forget
   the change of seasons
   and footsteps of ancient beasts,
   whose bones here entombed,
   once sensed the ebb and flow
   of distant mountains,
   and the drifting of a continent.

Badlands National Park

Wherefore ourselves,
momentary caretakers,
new forms from old parts
in the evolutionary strata
of eons.
Who, wrapped in the folds
of the future,
will gaze upon our badlands.

Badlands National Park

Badlands at Zabriskie Point,
Death Valley National Monument, California

Badlands National Park

Monks and priests
  in the amphitheater at sunrise,
  commemorating the events
  of their own creation,

Fragile forms
  in colorful robes
  etched by countless washings
  and the prying of many winters.

Bryce Canyon National Park, Utah

Sunrise in the badlands of Yellowstone Canyon,
Yellowstone National Park, Wyoming

Detail of badlands erosion

Zabriskie Point,
Death Valley National Monument

Dunescapes

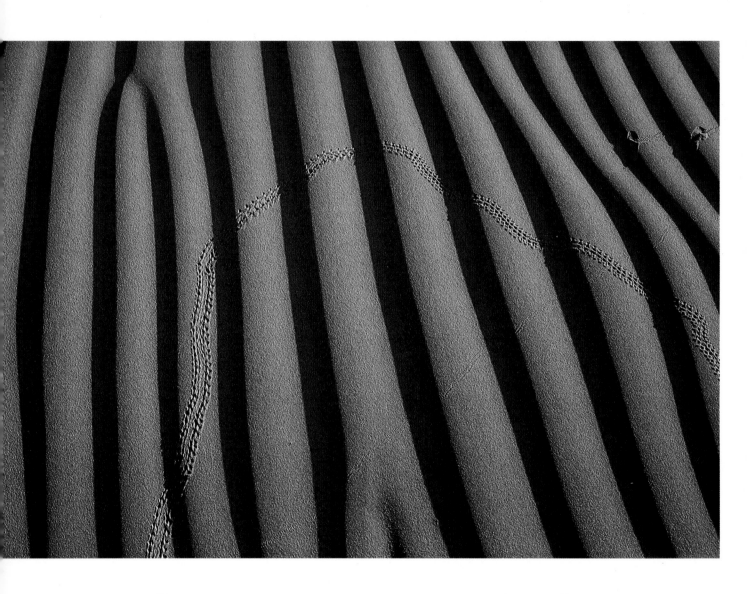

Ripple marks and dung beetle track in dune sand at Mesquite Flats,
Death Valley National Monument

Dunescapes

ALONE AMONG EARTH'S LANDFORMS, dunes are products of continual recreation. After a windstorm, illuminated by the brilliance of dawn or afterglow of sunset, they may exude such rare primordial beauty that it seems sacrilegious to tread upon them. Yet they beckon us with irresistible force. They are ethereal, permeated with a kind of mystical calm, a harmony of form. In their midst, we are spiritually refreshed and at peace. And in some inexplicable way, these same qualities often pervade our photographs.

Dunes form wherever a large supply of dry sand lies before relatively unrestrained wind. In addition to being a master shaper and piler, the wind is also a great sorter. Look closely at dune sand, and you will find the grains are all about the same size, the size that the wind moves most easily. Smaller, silt-size, grains are harder to break loose and send flying; but once in the air, they may remain in suspension for a long time and travel hundreds of miles before they settle. Larger particles, like pebbles, cobbles, and boulders, are too heavy to move and remain behind as lag gravel.

Sand accumulates wherever topography or vegetation interferes with the wind. The pile becomes asymmetrical as it builds because the wind drives the sand up the gentle windward side and over the crest. The lee side, meanwhile, steepens as new sand is added to its top until it reaches a maximum slope for the loose material. Then small landslides reduce the slope to a stable angle. Thus the backslope is called the slip face.

Saltation is responsible for the marvelous ripple patterns of sand dunes. Rippling takes place during gentle winds; when wind speed rises to about three times that necessary to start grains saltating, it flattens the ripples. If the wind dies away gradually, it may dump sand in the hollows between ripple crests. The uniform expanse of sharply-defined ripples so often seen covering large expanses of dunes, are products of a delicate balance between wind and gravity.

Formation of ripples is related to the shaping of the dunes themselves. Irregularities in the unrippled sand surface present one face toward and one face away from the wind. The windward face is subject to greater bombardment by bouncing sand grains, so that sand travels up that side, deepening the hollow in front and piling the sand onto or over a ripple crest. Creation of the ripple leaves a new hollow ahead of it, whose windward side is subject to similar bombardment. Since the sand grains are all about the same size, they follow similar trajectories, each leaping downwind about the same distance. Grains ejected from the base of one ripple land at the base of the next one, and those ejected from the ripple crest land at the next crest. In this way, the ripple wavelengths are adjusted to the length of the grain trajectory.

Sand migration on dunes creates a cross-bedding that may be preserved when the sand is converted to sandstone. Such is the case of the giant cross-beds in the petrified dunes of the Jurassic Navajo sandstone, now magnificently etched in relief by erosion in Zion Canyon, the Vermillion Cliffs near Grand Canyon, and other places in the American southwest. The beds are of two principal kinds: relatively thin, gently inclined, topset beds formed on the windward face of the dune, and the steeper, more numerous bottomset beds formed on the slip face. The topset beds are generally thinner because their materials are continually removed to the slip face. The bottomset beds, of course, are also destroyed in the process and new topset beds created from them; and the dune migrates downwind.

Dunes at Mesquite Flats,
Death Valley National Monument,
California

Dunes at Mesquite Flats,
Death Valley National Monument,
California

We are but dunes ourselves,
wrested from the barren land,
cast about from place to place
molded and remolded
by the winds of time.

Dunes at Mesquite Flats, Death Valley National Monument

A spirit dwells
*   among graceful windforms*
in a symphony of silence.

Wind ripples in dune sand at Mesquite Flats,
Death Valley National Monument

Playing among the frozen dunes
of Jurassic deserts,
giant cross-beds
echo howling winds
and shifting sands

Giant cross-beds in
Navajo sandstone,
Checkerboard Mesa,
Zion National Park,
Utah

Sand-sculptured mudcracks in a dune hollow at Mesquite Flats,
Death Valley National Monument, California

Playas

Death Valley salt pan, Death Valley National Monument, looking south toward Badwater

Playas

WHEN VIEWED FROM HIGH on the bordering mountainsides, Death Valley salt pan looks for all the world like a great frozen, snowclad lake, brilliantly reflecting the sun. From Dante's View, one mile above the east side of the pan, or from two miles above the west side on Telescope Peak, this impression may be greatly enhanced by the presence of snow underfoot. The impression, of course, is false. Instead, the "frozen lake" is just one of the most striking features of Death Valley National Monument, the hottest and driest part of the great Southwestern Desert. Summer temperatures on the valley floor average more than 100 degrees F. and have reached a maximum of 134 degrees, while annual precipitation averages only about 1.5 inches. Under these conditions, any runoff water that manages to veneer the valley floor as a shallow playa lake evaporates quickly, leaving dissolved minerals behind as a salt crust. Most of the salt here, however, comes from wetter times in the recent geologic past. There are thick deposits, for example, from a lake that filled the basin to 30 feet as recently as 4000-5000 years ago; beneath them lie thicker layers deposited from a 600-foot deep lake that existed during part of the Pleistocene or glacial epoch, a time when many large lakes occupied the valleys of the Basin and Range province.

Such deposits are called evaporites because they originate by evaporation of mineral-bearing waters. The minerals come from the rocks and soils over, or through which, the water flows. As the water evaporates, the dissolved salts concentrate until they begin to precipitate. The saturation level is different for each of the many different dissolved salts, but the order of precipitation in a gradually drying lake is from least soluble to most soluble: first, the carbonates, then the sulfates, and finally the chlorides such as rock salt.

Formation of the Death Valley salt pan from those ancient lakes can be likened to evaporation from a shallow dish with a curved bottom, in which salt water at first fills the dish to the brim. Of course, the wetted area shrinks as the water evaporates. At some point, carbonates precipitate, and they continue to coat the bottom until all are lost from solution. The pool is much smaller when sulfates begin to form a cap over the carbonates, and smaller yet when chlorides begin to come out. When all the water is gone, the dish would be crusted with salts, carbonates on the bottom and extending far up the sides, and chlorides topping all only in the middle of the dish. From the top the three groups of salt would present a bullseye pattern of concentric bands.

The analogy with Death Valley would be even better if the dish were tilted as the valley has been, so that the bands of exposed salt are narrower on the down side than on the up side. Drying of the ancient lakes was not perfectly uniform and gradual, and since the last one dried up, some surface areas have been repeatedly wetted and dried, subjected to intense weathering and erosion.

The resulting salt pan is a fantasyland of weird little landscapes, unlike any other in nature. Certainly the most striking part in Death Valley is the Devil's Golf Course, where mounds of silty salt up to about three feet high grew by crystallization of salts from rising groundwater. Wind and rain carved the mounds into an incredible maze of pinnacles, covered with sharp points that look like shark's teeth. Other areas of the pan are flat, gleaming white surfaces with polygonal patterns of ridges. The ridges are mudcracks filled with salt precipitated during periodic wetting. The cracks narrow downward, so the filling is wedge-shaped. The wedges grow sideways and upward with each wetting until they form rims around saucer-like depressions, each of which becomes a miniature salt pan when flooded again. Here and there are small depressions into salt-water pools where one can see extremely delicate, hair-like crystal growths.

Not all playas contain salt pans like these; the so-called Racetrack, in one of the more remote parts of the Death Valley National Monument illustrates the point. Here instead of salt is an extremely flat cake of dried and cracked mud. The Racetrack name refers to its moving stones. They fell onto the lakebed from bordering cliffs. When it rains enough to wet the surface, the mud becomes extremely slick, and the wind often blows at speeds of up to 70 miles per hour. Then the stones slide across the mud, leaving trails behind them. When the surface again dries, the trails may remain as a record of their travels.

Devils Golf Course, part
of the Death Valley salt pan

This is a strange land of contrasts,
  where tortured salt crusts
  writhe and groan
  in the shimmering heat
  and magnificent desolation
  of a treeless valley

Detail of salt crust in Devils Golf Course

Where the gleaming white pan
  gracefully blends
  into the brown slopes
  of alluvial fans
  at the foot of mountains
  with snow-clad summits.

Death Valley salt pan and the Funeral Mountains, looking north

Fine salt crystals by a water hole in the salt pan,
Death Valley National Monument

Mudcrack patterns in Death Valley salt pan

Racetrack playa, with Grandstand,
Death Valley National Monument

Mosaic of sliding rocks on the Racetrack playa,
Death Valley National Monument

Ice

"Wineglass" icicles, Raquette River in March,
Adirondack region, New York

Ice

THOSE OF US WHO LIVE in the high latitudes, or altitudes, know ice, the solid form of water, the only major substance capable of existing in its gaseous, liquid, and solid forms within the normal range of temperatures on the Earth's surface. The ease with which water passes from one state to the other is largely responsible for the incredible variety and beauty of ice forms. Ice crystallizes directly from vapor as well as from liquid and passes back into both states as easily. All the ice we see at the Earth's surface is crystalline. Ice expresses its internal crystalline structure in the intricate and infinitely variable hexagonal forms of snowflakes, elongate facets of filament ice on a freezing pond, delicate frost flowers, or icy filigree on a window. But the misshapen grains of "corn snow," hail, icicles, hoar frost, rime, and blue glacial ice are equally crystalline. They have an equally orderly, geometric, internal arrangement of hydrogen-oxygen molecules. Each grain is a separate crystal, but their crowding prevents external expression of facets like those of a snowflake.

Ice is also rock, with all of the characteristics of its harder, and more durable counterparts: igneous, sedimentary, and metamorphic rocks. Metamorphic ice rock forms in glaciers that move like rivers, and in which the ice crystals are densely packed under the weight of the overlying material.

Ice is the only natural rock that flows significantly at the Earth's surface under its own weight. In so doing, the rock also deforms as do harder rocks subjected to the more severe conditions deep within the crust. Many large, active mountain glaciers in Alaska, the Alps, and elsewhere, carry long, sinous stripes of rocky moraine that record the downward flow of the ice over hundreds of years. From afar, they look for all the world like giant ribbon candy.

Wind-sculptured snow comes in many interesting forms, including dunes, hollows, and sastrugi that closely resemble dunescapes and textures of the desert. Cornices are smoothly-curved and tenuous snow overhangs formed where the wind blows over a dunecrest or ridge of some kind. Wind and sun together often etch snow surfaces into a tiny forest of skeletal forms. Even more intricate and frail are the textural mazes of old snow subjected for several days to the freeze-dry effect of bright sun and sub-freezing temperatures without wind.

Ice sculpture is at its best in Spring, when the temperature hovers near freezing, creating unbelievably delicate dripstone and flowstone structures like those of limestone caves; but these are crystal-clear ice in needle-like icicles and paper-thin "drapes" that refract the sunlight and sparkle like diamonds. These are only a few examples from the gallery of ice art; there is much more. Let the pictures speak.

Ice on window,
-20 degrees F.

Ice on window, -20 degrees F.

Stalactites and delicate frost crystals at -30 degrees F.,
west branch St. Regis River, Adirondack region

Ice "chimes," Raquette River in March,
Adirondack region

Ice saucers on Grass River,
Adirondack Mountains

Frozen waterfall, Oswegatchie River, Adirondack region

Frost flowers, -30 degrees F.

Ice, snow, water at Lampson Falls, Grass River,
Adirondack region

Rime ice and snow at the high falls of Chateaugay River,
Adirondack region

Rime ice and snow
at the high falls of
Chateaugay River,
Adirondack Region

Ice along West Branch St. Regis River,
Adirondack Mountains

Icicles on rock,
Whiteface
Memorial Highway,
Adirondack Mountains

Spring breakup, west branch St. Regis River, Adirondack region

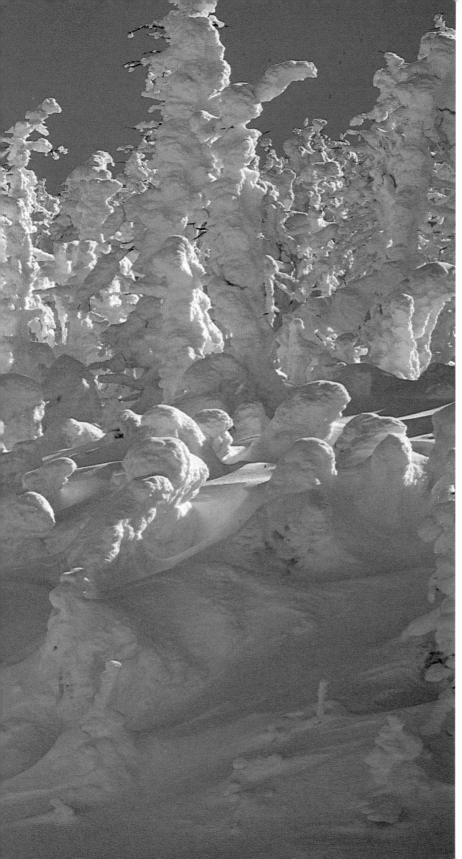

Rime and snow near timberline
on Whiteface Mountain,
Adirondack Mountains

The Art of Pele

New growth in old pahoehoe lava, Hawaii Volcanoes National Park,
on the big island of Hawaii

The Art of Pele

OF ALL THE GEOLOGIC PROCESSES we can observe directly, volcanic eruptions must surely be the most awesome and inspiring. An eruption is a catastrophic event that can create or destroy an entire mountain in a moment of geologic time. For example, the island of Surtsey, off the south coast of Iceland, emerged from the sea in less than a week after violent submarine eruptions began November 14, 1963. On the other hand, Mt. St. Helens, once one of the world's loveliest mountains, was practically obliterated in the blink of an eye by the cataclysmic eruption of May 18, 1980. That event was just one of hundreds, even thousands, that have at times built up, and at other times, torn down the mountain during the last 40,000 years.

Of course, not all volcanism is so violent. Kilauea, on the big island of Hawaii, is one of the most active volcanoes in the world. When it erupts, as it is doing at the moment I write this, lava may first jet into the air in glowing fountains, then it flows down the mountain like water, sometimes at speeds in excess of 30 miles per hour, forming streams, cascades, ponds, and sheet-like floods that cover many square miles. Geologists refer to this very liquid lava and its solid counterpart by the Hawaiian name, Pahoehoe.

Pahoehoe can't flow forever because it cools and stiffens rapidly. When the lava slows down, it moves like thick molasses and drags against obstacles — trees, rocks, old lava flows — so that the surface folds over itself and becomes twisted and ropey. A crust forms, and here and there, still-liquid lava may break through to form bulbous "tongues" or "toes." The final product is a convoluted, tangled mass that often resembles black spaghetti—Pele pasta.

After they harden, Pahoehoe lavas shine like burnished ebony because a thin veneer of glass, the product of quick quenching of the lava against the air, coats the surface. At closer range, the glass reflects and refracts the bright island sun into millions of pinpoints of varicolored light.

Aa is the Hawaiian name for a stiffer type of lava that almost invariably follows Pahoehoe in a single eruptive episode. Although it may be compositionally similar to Pahoehoe, it is cooler and forms thicker, slower, and heavily-crusted flows. Continued movement of viscous lava within rafts the crust and breaks it up into large "klinkery" blocks that pile up in front, alongside, and on top of the flow. The final product is a forbidding jumble of spiny, dull black rock. Where youthful Aa and Pahoehoe flows overlap each other, they contrast strikingly.

Haleakala of the island of Maui is another kind of volcano. From its summit at 10,000 feet above the sea, you may survey a seven-mile-long depression studded with near-perfect, cratered cinder cones. They are painted with an amazing variety of muted pastel colors, products of reactions between volcanic gases and the erupted rocks. Add, here and there, the subtle greens of the sparse vegetation, and you have an unusual pallet for such a barren landscape.

Puu o Maui, Kamaolii, Kaluu o Ka Oo, Pau o Pele, Ka Moa o Pele, Halalii, Puu Naue, Puu Maile, Oili Puu — the exotic names of the cinder cones sound like a Hawaiian chant. They are silent now, but their forms reveal violent eruptions too recent for erosion to have creased their slopes. Much of the giant summit crater they occupy is strewn with the ash, cinders, and volcanic bombs, the missiles of those violent events. Among the deposits are incredibly smooth, curved slopes of velvety silver-gray ash. In less-protected places, the wind has selectively carried away the ash and left behind a virtual pavement of bombs, in places so evenly distributed that they appear to have been arranged by hand.

Haleakala crater is an anomaly. Rather than an eruptive center, the present depression is really the product of erosion during a long lapse of volcanic activity that preceded the cinder cone eruptions. Rivers then eroded the sides of the mountain; the headwaters of two of the most vigorous ones, Koolau and Kaupo, cut so deeply that they met at the summit and carved out the crater. They are now separated by only a narrow, low divide in the mid-section of the crater.

Erosion of volcanoes may produce exotic landforms. For

example, the startling monolith called Shiprock juts 1700 feet above the flat desert floor in northwestern New Mexico, looking for all the world like a giant sailing ship in a calm sea. This is a volcanic neck standing high after erosion has stripped away the softer rocks that once enclosed it. According to one interpretation, the mountain originally projected from a surface much higher than the present one, perhaps even higher than the summit of Shiprock. Several striking dikes of black igneous rock that radiate from Shiprock, and stand like ruined walls above the plain, formed as lava filled tensional fractures.

Yellowstone Park is a showcase of simmering volcanism where the last eruptions occurred about 600,000 years ago. The region abounds in lava flows and colorful deposits of volcanic tephra, the ash-cinder-bomb conglomeration of explosive eruptions. In the walls of Yellowstone Canyon are pastel colors similar to those of Haleakala and produced in the same way: by reactions between the erupted debris and the highly corrosive gases that pass through them.

Above all, Yellowstone is a place of geysers, erupting hot springs that occur where hot magma lies at shallow depth, where there is a plentiful supply of water, and where open passageways perforate the rocks. Under just the right conditions, superheated groundwater erupts as it flashes into steam at regular or irregular intervals. Yellowstone claims about 62 per cent of the world's geysers, as well as thousands of hot springs, mud pots, and fumaroles.

The geysers and hot springs are sites of unusual and often colorful deposits, geyserite or travertine. The difference is that the geyserite is principally composed of silica, and the travertine of calcium carbonate, the stuff of limestone. Each is dissolved from the rocks the hot water passes through. If the rocks are siliceous, the water dissolves silica, but if the rocks are limestone, it dissolves calcium carbonate. When the hot water issues to the surface, the minerals quickly precipitate, forming tiered pools and mounds of flowstone like those often seen in caves.

The marriage of Pele, goddess of earth and fire, and Kama-puaa, god of water, was short and violent. In a rage, she routed him from her crater of fire and chased him with streams of lava into the sea.

Hawaiian legend

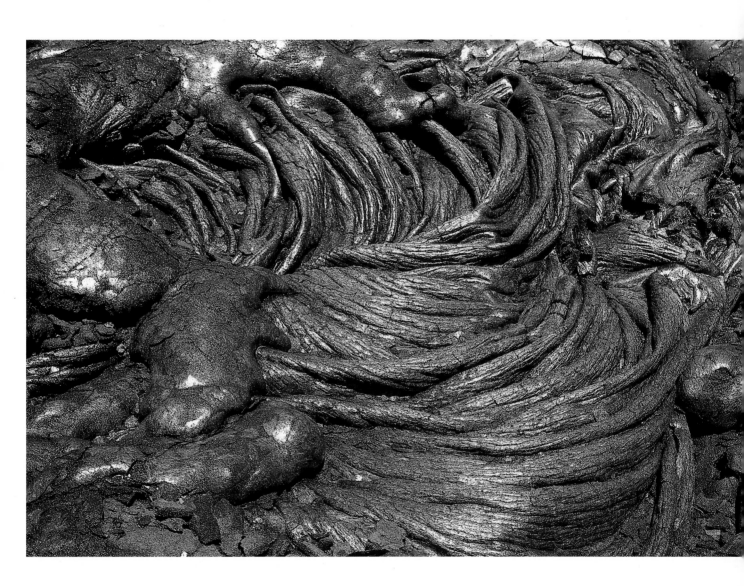

Pahoehoe lava, Hawaii Volcanoes National Park

Renewal.
   Nestled in a crease
   between pahoehoe billows,
   life begins anew,
   unknowing
   that beneath these frozen liquid forms
   rest countless others like them
   foretelling
   eruptions yet to come.

Now Pele rests.

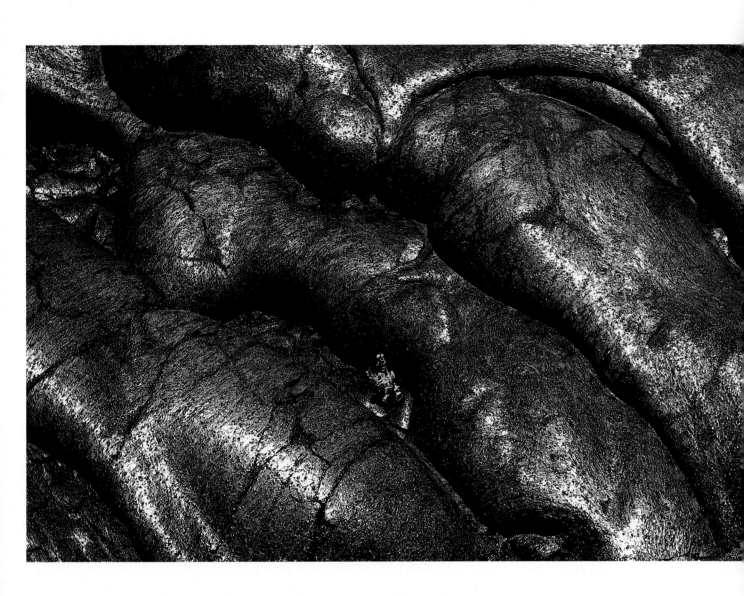

Pahoehoe lava, Hawaii Volcanoes National Park

Summit region of Haleakala volcano,
with cinder cones,
Haleakala National Park,
on the island of Maui

Standing there in the cold wind
near the south dike,
I watch the dawning sun
touch the sails of this grand ship,
as my thoughts go back twenty four years,
when we struggled for the topmost pinnacle
in the long shadows of another morning

Now it appears unchanged,
but I know it cannot be.
How crumbly the rock was then, as now,
a chaos of volcanic tuff
with blocks of lava, sandstone, shale, and even granite,
rent from the walls
in the deep throat of the volcano
by cataclysmic eruptions.

The cone,
and the thick sedimentary rock floor
upon which it rested,
are gone now,
victims of inexorable erosion;
all that remains
is this muted frozen voice.

Shiprock, New Mexico

In her reverie,
      she stood upon the slope
      of an obscure mountain valley
      looking down upon terraced ricepaddies
      that climbed the opposite wall.

Then, a child's voice
      suddenly awakened her to the reality
      of tiered pools of hot water
      with siliceous sinter dams
      at one of Yellowstone's boiling caldrons.

Tiered siliceous sinter of hot spring,
Yellowstone National Park, Wyoming

Algal-bacteria stringers in hot pool at Mammoth Hot Springs,
Yellowstone National Park

Mammoth Hot Springs, Yellowstone National Park

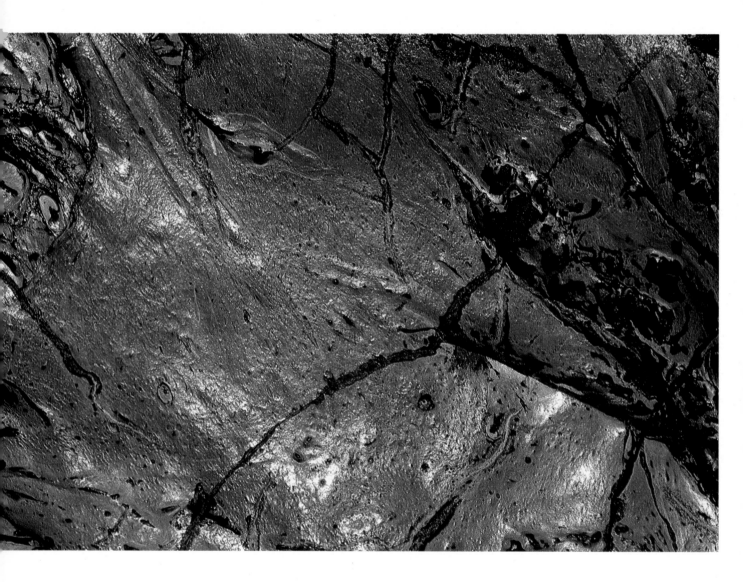

Hardened lava, Kilauea caldera, Hawaii Volcanoes National Park

Spheroidally weathered basalt near Grand Coulee, Washington

Microcosms

Actinolite in randomly-oriented, intergrown crystals

Microcosms

ONE OF THE BASIC TOOLS of geology is the polarizing microscope. Using light transmitted through very thin slices of rocks, this instrument reveals an amazing world of abstract realism. Most rocks are aggregates of different minerals. Each of the hundreds of different minerals is constructed of atoms and molecules fitted together in a repetitive geometric pattern. On the stage of the polarizing microscope, this internal structure gives each mineral grain unique shape and color, which enables geologists to identify individual species.

Most of the color is interference color. White light that enters the crystal is a mixture of all the colors of the rainbow. Passage through the mineral and the microscope polarizers sorts these colors out, eliminates some, and mixes the remainder in different proportions, creating a wide variety of brilliant hues.

Interference color is controlled in part by grain orientation with respect to the transmitted light path. A rock thin section commonly contains hundreds of grains of a particular mineral, each with a different orientation so that each grain displays unique color. Turn the microscope stage, and each grain also fades, blinks, and brightens, producing a kaleidoscopic effect.

Now add numerous grains each of several other mineral species that make up the rock, each having its own interference color, each with its own orientation, and each blinking on and off in its own time — a moving feast of color.

Add form, the external expression of the internal atomic order referred to as "crystal." Everyone knows what a crystal is; it has flat, shiny faces that join at sharp angles and combine into distinctive shapes. The faces follow certain atomic planes of the internal structure, and thus they reveal the structure without the aid of X-ray or electron microscope. The crystal structure is always there; whether the face develops or not largely depends on the freedom of growth. Lavas commonly contain large, well-defined crystals "floating" in a fine-grained groundmass. The crystals grew freely, and slowly, in a liquid environment. When the lava erupted, the remaining melt cooled too fast for other large crystals to form; and the early crystals were frozen in place — suspended in time.

Cleavage is the ability of a mineral to break easily along certain atomic planes as in mica. Cleavage is often conspicuous under the microscope, but difficult to see otherwise — and this also adds to the hidden art of the microcosm. For example, amphibole has two directions of perfect cleavage planes that lend an attractive diamond-shaped grid pattern — in grains that are properly oriented to the collage of color and form.

Twinning occurs when two or more parts of a crystal intergrow in certain ways, again determined by the atomic architecture of the mineral. A simple twin may have two parts that are mirror images of each other. Under the microscope, the two parts are often sharply separated; each displays its own interference color and blinks in its own time. Some twinned crystals have several parts, giving striped, radial, or other patterns.

Add zoning. Many minerals have variable chemical composition that affects their color and texture under the microscope. For example, plagioclase feldspar growing in a basaltic lava tends to incorporate more calcium at high temperatures and more sodium at low temperatures. If the cooling rate is just right, a marvelously, intricately zoned crystal will grow. Under the microscope you may see a grain with numerous concentric internal crystal outlines marking the zone boundaries, perfectly formed crystals within perfectly formed crystals. Each zone has its own optical orientation, and each blinks independently.

All these elements combine in the microcosm to an infinite variety of abstract art. The result sometimes is just a melange of interlocking grains, each with its distinctive geometry, but with little color. In other cases, it is a gourmet feast of patterns, form, and color of incredible brilliance. The possibilities are endless.

Forsterite olivine
with chrysotile
serpentine alteration

Olivine
with many
irregular fractures

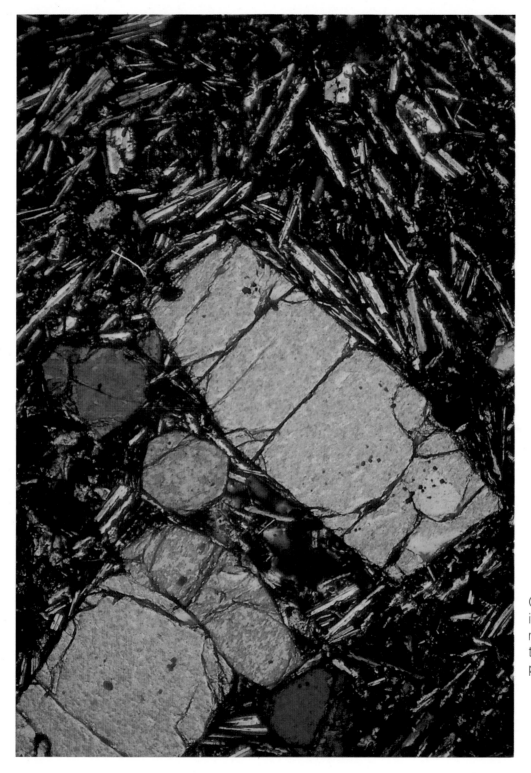

Olivine crystals
in fine-grained
matrix containing
tiny laths of
plagioclase feldspar

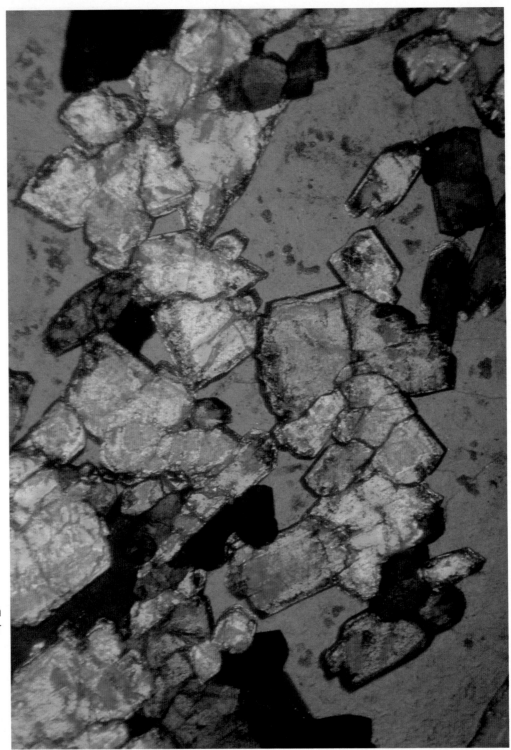

Epidote crystals in
plagioclase feldspar

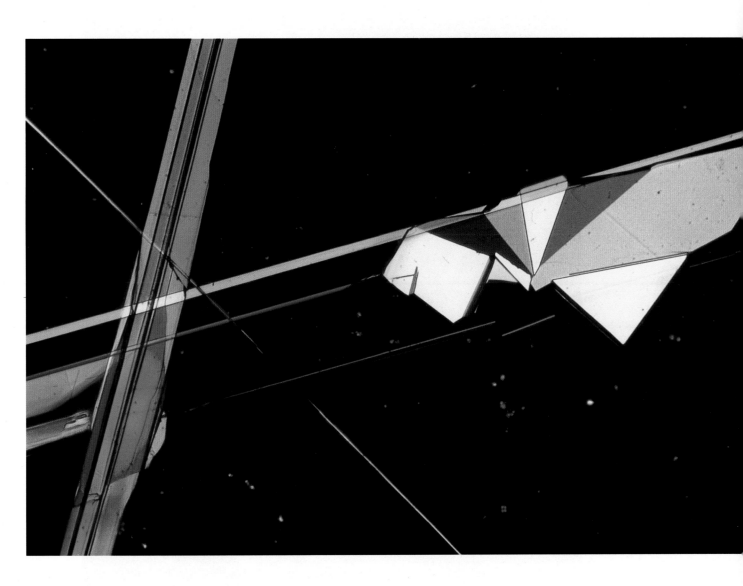

Rutile crystals in phlogopite mica

Rutile crystals
in phlogopite mica

Prehnite

Prehnite

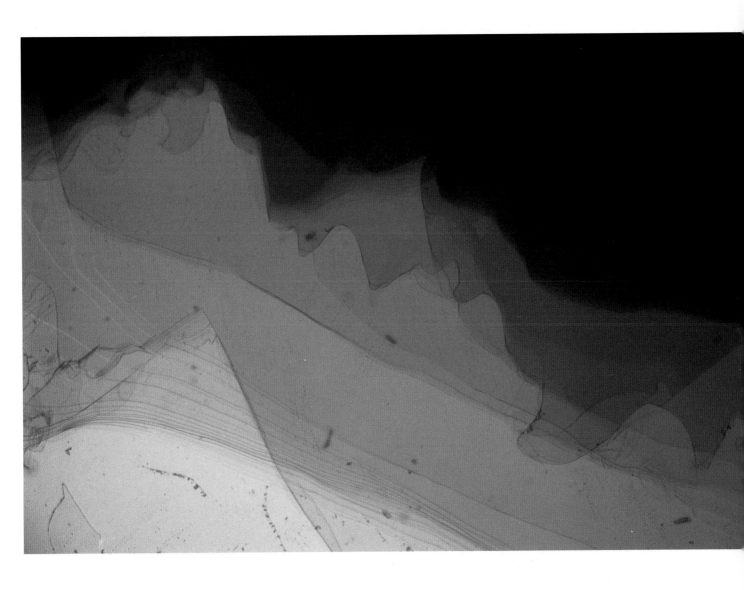

Muscovite

Muscovite

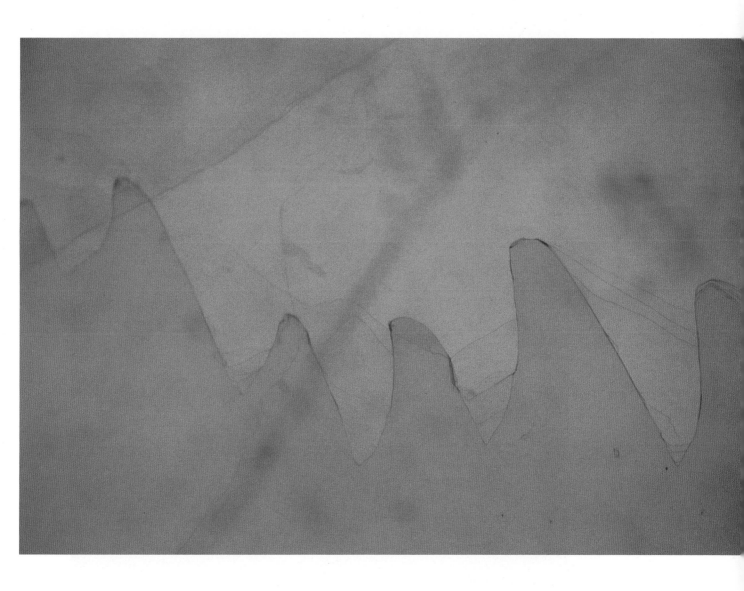

Muscovite

High Falls Gorge
on the west branch
Ausable River,
Adirondack Mts. ,
carved into
Wilmington Notch
fault zone

Other Places Other Times

The mystique of the glens
is less of dark shadows,
hidden crevices and hollows,
than of voices in stone
untouched by the sun
for 350 million years.

Watkins Glen,
Finger Lakes region,
New York,
at the south end
of the Seneca Lake
glacial trough

Now, the river trickles by
      while pollen-dusted pools
reflect smooth potholes
and hide round-worn pestel stones.

Solid evidence
      that within the spring chaos
      the hand of Nature is graceful.

Pothole in the riverbed just below the Isabella Lake dam, California

Reflecting upon the meaning
of steep valley sides
and rounded distant hills.
I ride the crest of ice, not stone,
that gouges, scours, and shapes
this scene of tranquil beauty
from reluctant rock.

Indian Head ledges
above Lower
Ausable Lake,
Adirondack Mountains

Balanced Rock section
of Arches National Park, Utah

143

There is something sad
and something wonderful
about erosion.
It destroys,
while it builds
beautiful new worlds,
if only for a moment.

Karst topography along the river Li near Guilin, China

The Matterhorn,
bold imprint of time,
yet ephemeral, suspended
between creation and decay,
rocks born of long-gone seas,
tortured and thrust on high,
sculptured by wind, water, and ice.

For one who knows Earth,
to climb the Matterhorn
is to touch the past
and see the future.
Each handhold, layer, crystal,
boulder, pinnacle, crevice
screams of history.

And from the summit
Nature's boundless splendor
inspires wonder, mystery, awe,
and over all,
a false sense of power.
Yet this perch, as humanity's,
is but one step from oblivion.
Knowing that, I, at least, tread with care
and know peace.

The Swiss summit of the Matterhorn as seen from the Italian summit

About the photographs:

I took all of the scenic photographs with a Nikon F2AS 35 mm camera with one of three Nikkor lenses: 55 mm F 3.5 Micro-Nikkor, a 28 mm F 2.8 wide angle, and 80-200 mm F 4.5 Zoom. I used Ektachrome 100, processed by Richard L. Bitely of the State University of New York College at Potsdam, and Kodachrome 64, processed by Kodak. I used a Zeiss Photomicroscope and Ektachrome 150 (tungsten) film for the photomicrographs; these were also processed by Dick Bitely.

List of photographs

MICROCOSMS

120. Actinolite in randomly-oriented, intergrown crystals
123. Forsterite olivine with chrysotile serpentine alteration
124. Olivine with many irregular fractures
125. Olivine crystals in fine-grained matrix
     containing tiny laths of plagioclase feldspar
126. Epidote crystals in plagioclase feldspar
127. Rutile crystals in phlogopite mica
128. Rutile crystals in phlogopite mica
129. Prehnite
130. Prehnite
131. Muscovite
132. Muscovite
133. Muscovite

OTHER PLACES, OTHER TIMES

134. High Falls Gorge on the west branch Ausable River, Adirondack Mts.,
     New York, carved into Wilmington Notch fault zone
137. Watkins Glen, Finger Lakes region, New York,
     at the south end of the Seneca Lake glacial trough
139. Pothole in the riverbed just below the Isabella Lake dam, California
141. Indian Head ledges above Lower Ausable Lake,
     Adirondack Mountains
142-43. Balanced Rock section of Arches National Park, Utah
145. Karst topography along the river Li near Guilin, China
147. The Swiss summit of the Matterhorn as seen from the Italian summit